The E

Cotswold
Walks

by

Christopher Knowles

Family walks of between 3 and 5 miles, including
places of refreshment along the way.

REARDON & SON
CHELTENHAM, ENGLAND

Published
by
REARDON PUBLISHING
56, Upper Norwood Street, Leckhampton,
Cheltenham, Glos, GL53 0DU, England
Website: www.reardon.co.uk

ISBN 1 873877 03 X

Written and Researched by
Christopher Knowles
for
The Cheltenham Newspaper Company Ltd

Maps, Illustrations, Layout and Design
by
Peter Reardon

Printed by
In2Print Ltd,
Cheltenham

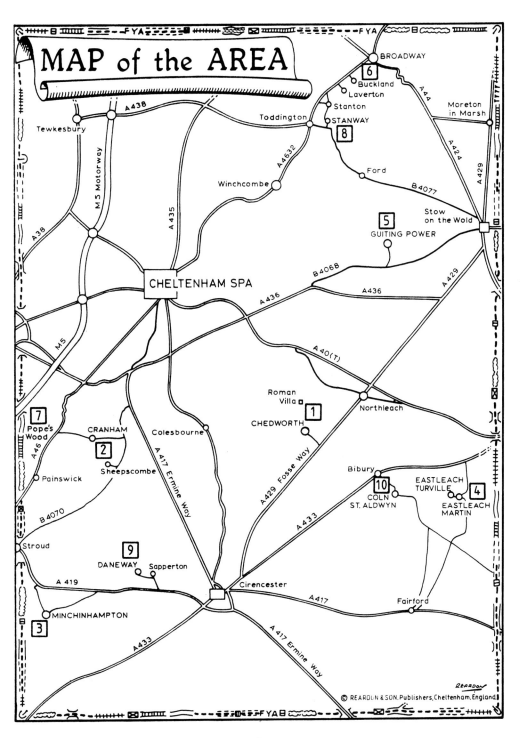

MAP of the AREA

BROADWAY

6

Buckland
Laverton
Stanton

Moreton
in Marsh

A44

Tewkesbury

A438

Toddington

STANWAY

8

A46 32

Ford

B4077

A424

A429

M5 Motorway

A435

Winchcombe

Stow
on the Wold

5

GUITING POWER

A38

B4068

A429

CHELTENHAM SPA

A436

A436

M5

A40(T)

Roman
Villa

1

CHEDWORTH

Northleach

7

Pope's
Wood

CRANHAM

Colesbourne

A46

2

Sheepscombe

Bibury

A429 Fosse Way

EASTLEACH
TURVILLE

4

Painswick

A417 Ermine Way

10

COLN
ST. ALDWYN

EASTLEACH
MARTIN

B4070

A433

Stroud

9

DANEWAY

Sapperton

Cirencester

A417

Fairford

A419

3

MINCHINHAMPTON

A433

A417 Ermine Way

1. Chedworth

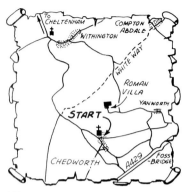

Distance: $3\frac{3}{4}$ miles
Time: $2/2\frac{1}{4}$ hours of uninterrupted walking
Map: In the OS Pathfinder series you need SP 01/11 Northleach and Andoversford
Starting Point: Grid Ref 052122. Chedworth Church
Terrain: Mostly track and woodland path with some field and a little road walking. The going is reasonably firm but you might meet a little mud from time to time. The gentle undulations are hardly taxing.
Refreshments: excellent food at the very attractive Seven Tuns pub in Chedworth.

THIS walk begins and ends in the village of Chedworth, taking you above this charming village and then down through woodland to a Roman villa. It continues by meadows and a meandering river and returns through graceful woodland and across fields to Chedworth and an ancient inn.

Turn right from Chedworth church down towards the lower road and take the little path on your left that will bring you out onto the road below opposite the pub, the Seven Tuns.

Turn left here and walk along the road until you quickly meet Corner Cottage, with a red pillar box of Queen Victoria vintage, set in its wall. Turn left here along a narrow road which rises gently. Soon stone walls will appear on either side. By some cottages of comparatively recent construction to the right, signs indicate a public footpath and Chedworth Roman Villa. Take this road which passes between cottages to left and right and quickly ends at a metal gate with a stile. The church sits majestically above you to the back and the village rests snugly below you.

The stile brings you into a narrow field. Keep to its left hand margin, next to a stone wall, as it curves around to the left. Ahead of you is a long two storey farmhouse beneath a low ridge. As you move forward the field opens up to the left. You should head for the top right corner of the field, just to the left of the farmhouse. In the area of this corner there is a cluster of gates and stiles, each marked with a yellow arrow. One is a little to the left, beneath one of the taller trees; another on the right, bears a sign for Chedworth Villa and appears to lead into a paddock. Ignore both and take the one in the middle and bear right around the outside of the paddock until you meet, after thirty yards or so, another stile that leads onto a grassy bank. In fact there is a double set of stiles here, with something that looks like a sluice gate between the two. Proceed along the grassy bank, with the farmhouse just below you to the right, until you come to a bridle gate on the left. Go through this and gird yourself for the short climb up a small field towards a small stile, with the house behind you and beyond it, the church.

Here you will find yourself on a wider track and a choice of directions to go in. In fact you want the least likely looking path - not the one on the extreme left, or the one on the extreme right; nor the one straight ahead of you but the one that leads away diagonally to the left, between two wooden huts behind a wire fence to the left and stone wall to the right and which seems to disappear into thicket.

4

The track soon narrows to a path and falls away into the woodland. You will arrive at a crossroads of paths but carry straight on into the woods, following a bridleway sign. The path continues to descend until it meets a wall and curves away to the left with the bulk of the Chedworth Woods, some of the oldest in the Cotswolds, to the right. Pass through the remains of a gateway into the wood proper and follow the path as it continues to descend with the body of the wood, a tangle of undergrowth around an assortment of trees, spread over broad banks on both sides.

Eventually the path flattens out and meets another path but will sweep you naturally to the right towards a sort of clearing of thinly spread trees. You are at the edge of the wood now, views opening up to the right towards the Coln Valley. Ignore one track leading off to the right down towards a cottage but keep to the track on the margin of the wood, going more or less straight on as it leads up and narrows towards a wooden gate. Go through this and on to a metalled road.

By turning left here you will arrive, after about 100 yards, at Chedworth Roman Villa, considered by many to be the most attractive in Britain. It was discovered in 1864 by a ferret whose enthusiasm for the hunt forced his owner to dig him out, in the process of which pieces of mosaic were found. It is possible that the villa originally stood in open or cultivated countryside for much woodland had been cleared by the time of the arrival of the Romans in Britain, only reappearing with the Saxons. The villa is now owned by the National Trust and has a small museum. Winter opening hours are limited - ring Withington 256 to check.

After your visit return to where you joined the road from Chedworth Woods - before you is the Coln Valley. Keep to the road as it continues down and soon meets a crossroads. The road continues to Yanworth and Northleach; to the left another goes to Cheltenham and Withington. But you turn to the right through the green gate, with Private Road - Footpath Only sign attached to it, on to a wide, level and firm track that passes through an avenue of trees.

The track soon passes a cottage on the right and then the woods. On the left is a meadow with the River Coln meandering prettily through it and, beyond, more woodland ranged up a bank.

The river soon finds its way to the track you are following and accompanies it in an almost straight line through rushes and reeds. Keep to the track until its natural end, taking care not to enter the woods on the right which are private. After a while the river careers away again to follow a wilder course through an open field dotted with a few trees as the woodland gives ground to cultivated hillside. Then the woodland re-establishes itself and begins to nip in a little from the left as the track comes to an end at another green gate and a bend in a metalled road. To your left the road leads across a small bridge to a mill. To your right is a cottage.

Walk straight on past the cottage when you will immediately see a small low stile leading into the woods. Take this and climb up and slightly to the left - the path is just about obvious. Carry straight on at a crossroads and continue to the top of a bank that leads down to a low, shallow valley. Bear right here, keeping to the line of the bank, following the valley and ignoring all paths leading back into the main part of the wood. The walking is good here through airy woodland, with high, well spread trees.

The valley begins to close in as you approach the edge of the wood. The path is not very clear at this juncture but if you keep just to the right of the valley you should find a way over the remains of a stone wall into a field. There is a spring here too, so a trickle of water will tell you that you are on the right course. To your right, on the edge of the wood, is a small cottage. To your left, beyond the wood, is a road.

There is a footpath sign here pointing across the field towards a solitary tree near the top of the slope - you may even be able to see the impression of a path. Head for the tree. When you reach it turn right and head across the field taking a slightly diagonal path that keeps you to the left of the most distant outcrop of woodland. This will bring you to the edge of the field by a stone wall. Behind you are good views across the woodland you have emerged from to the valley beyond. Cross the wall - at this point you want to head across the field before you to a tree on the corner of a grassy track where two (hedgeless) fields meet, to the right of a farm building. After that go straight ahead and enter a defile on a corner with hedge on the left and wire fence to the right. Of course if the path across the field is not clear, especially when it is under cultivation, the same effect can be achieved by turning left out of the woods and following the perimeter of the field alongside the road until you meet the farm building where you should turn right to rejoin the path.

This leads to a gate - go through this until you come to a point you should recognise, a junction of paths with the farmhouse below, and beyond it to Chedworth. Turn left here and follow the track to a metalled road where you turn right. Follow the road down to the village and the Seven Tuns.

On the Way

The Church of St. Andrew, Chedworth, dates back in part (the lower part of the tower, the font and nave arcade) to about 1100, although there was a church on the site at the time of the Norman Conquest. Alterations and enlargements were made in the 13th and 15th centuries. Worthy of particular note are the font, the fine range of perpendicular windows on the south side, the 15th century stone pulpit and the sculpture of the Virgin and Child of 1911. A more detailed history is available for a small sum in the church.

The CHEDWORTH Walk

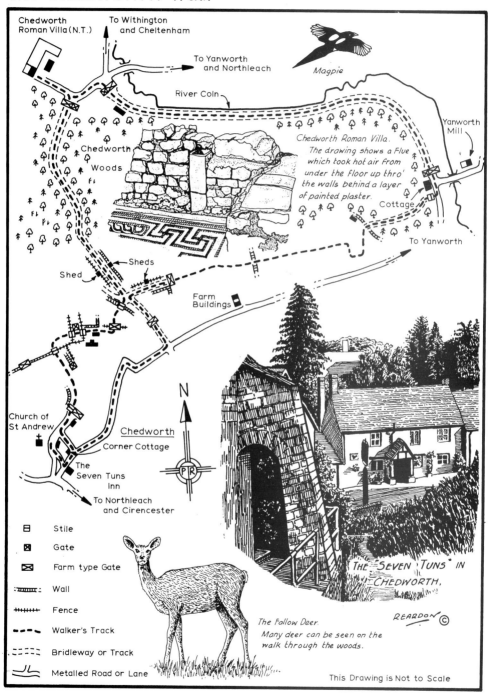

Chedworth
Roman Villa (N.T.)

To Withington
and Cheltenham

To Yanworth
and Northleach

Magpie

River Coln

Chedworth Roman Villa.
The drawing shows a Flue
which took hot air from
under the floor up thro'
the walls behind a layer
of painted plaster.

Chedworth
Woods

Yanworth
Mill

Cottage

To Yanworth

Sheds

Shed

Farm
Buildings

N

Church of
St Andrew

Chedworth

Corner Cottage

The
Seven Tuns
Inn

To Northleach
and Cirencester

THE "SEVEN TUNS" IN
CHEDWORTH,

REARDON ©

	Stile
	Gate
	Farm type Gate
	Wall
	Fence
	Walker's Track
	Bridleway or Track
	Metalled Road or Lane

The Fallow Deer.
Many deer can be seen on the
walk through the woods.

This Drawing is Not to Scale

2. Cranham/Sheepscombe

Distance: 3½ miles
Time: 2/2½ hours of uninterrupted walking
Map: OS Pathfinder series — SO 81/21
Starting Point: Grid Ref 894126
Terrain: Mostly track and woodland path and a little field walking. The going is reasonably firm but some mud inevitable in periods of rain. This is not a demanding walk. Some grazing animals in the open areas — dogs should be on leads.
Refreshments: There are two pubs within striking distance, the Black Horse at Cranham and the Butcher's Arms at Sheepscombe.

THIS walk starts and finishes in the village of Cranham, not far from Painswick, and takes you briskly across common and through high woodland to the edge of the village of Sheepscombe, where refreshment may be obtained from the local pub. Both Sheepscombe and Cranham have literary associations; and both have interesting churches.

Park off the road near the school at Cranham. If you wish to take a look at Cranham Church, with its very attractive interior, walk right (as you look at the school) for a short distance. The church is on the left. Mostly 15th century, it has several notable features – a 16th century rood screen, a fine monument to the long-serving 18th century rector, Obadiah Done, and a handsome altar tryptych. That sheep have long played a part in local life is clear from the shears carved on the tower.

The walk, however, begins by taking a brown track that leads on to Cranham Common to the left of the school (as you look at it). Behind you is a valley of pasture, concealing Painswick Stream, and woodland and stone houses. After about 40 yards you come to another track leading up and over the common but you turn hard right and follow the track as it passes behind the school and several other houses of recent vintage, with the common to the left. Very soon the path changes to concrete and descends. Below, in front of the woods (your first destination), there is a curiously well manicured meadow and Brook Farm, a trout farm. The path curves down towards it but just before you reach the farm entrance, you will see a path leading away to the left marked with posts dipped in yellow paint. Take this, proceeding through a gate after about 20 yards with the farm to the right and woodland above you to the left. The track may already be muddy. You will hear the sound of rushing water in front of you as the path descends and curves to the right over the stream which gushes picturesquely from the wood to the left into a holding pond right, pours down a plughole and comes to rest in the lake. The path now rises gently towards a gate, with the manicured field to the right.

The gate leads into Saltridge Wood, part of the Cotswold Commons and Beechwoods National Nature Reserve with some fine examples of ancient beechwood. The path ascends, with undergrowth on either side, skates along the edge of the wood and then cuts back in as it levels out. Soon you will notice another path joining from behind on the left but keep going forward. The path climbs slightly, edging a little to the right. Then you meet a rather complicated crossroads. Take the left-most path which slopes up through the trees, which may be marked with blue arrows. This path ascends sharply and levels out into a small clearing where another path comes in from behind on the left and another plunges down to the right; but you continue upwards and straight on through tall trees that rear above you out of bramble and holly on the bank to the left and descend in good order below you to the right, giving hints of good views. Finally, at the edge of the wood, the path levels out at a sort of crossroads with a stone wall in front of you. Here you bear left, keeping the wall to your left and the wood to your right. You should now keep to this path for some time, ignoring all paths leading back into the woods.

On the other side of the wall is a field, and the sky. As you continue the view opens up, with tree tops peeking over the horizon. The fields are symmetrical and well ordered, dotted with a few copses and larger areas of woodland. The path meanwhile begins to descend; beyond the wall, and across the field, you will see a stone gateway, presumably to Ebworth House. As the path begins to make a rather more rapid descent you will find yourself at another crossroads. Ahead of you are two gateways, the one on the left clearly marked 'Private'. Take the other, which is without a gate, and which leads to the edge of another wood. There you will see a sign marked 'National Trust, Lord's and Lady's Woods'. Turn left and take the path leading into the wood; almost immediately you will meet another fork – take the one on the right that leads downwards (you are still likely to find blue arrows indicating the way).

The path slopes down among the trees reasonably quickly, passing another National Trust sign on the right – ignore a downward path on the right and follow your path as it begins to ascend. Soon you can see a field through the trees on the left, seemingly provided with a cricket pavilion. Ahead of you a valley appears, and the beginning of a village. You are then confronted by a choice of paths, the lesser of the two, on the right, leading down to the village of Sheepscombe and the Butcher's Arms, the other, main path leading out of the wood and skirting it to the left. Unless you are descending to the village, take this.

Thus you emerge from the wood on to a platform of rough grass which falls away in a series of small, irregular terraces to the village below. The view from here is magnificent, not for its grandeur, but for its variety of character. Far away to the right, you can see the spire of Painswick. Between the two places are small, uneven fields, scattered with trees. Woodland covers the slope overlooking Sheepscombe, its crest a straight spine lined with a row of bristle like trees. Follow the track around the wood to the left. You will meet another track leading to a gate and field on the left – ignore this and carry on straight as the track starts to descend, a little scrubby here, with a few trees to the left. Soon houses are visible ahead. Just before the first of them, which marks the part of Sheepscombe known as Far End, take a narrow path, left, that leads up to a metal gate and stile, which lets you into the apex of a field.

Walk straight on, close to the edge and thin woodland on the right and then a modern house of unusual design with a tennis court. After about 150 yards you will see a stile in the top right corner which leads you onto a woodland path. This is Workmans Wood, also part of the National Nature Reserve. On your right the trees slope away and to the left they slope up – you are on a wide ledge between the two. Within 100 yards you will come to another path which you cross going diagonally upwards on the other side of it.

After 200 yards the path is joined by another but you carry on in the same direction. A stone wall will appear, left, beyond which is open ground; on your right, below, is a bowl of woodland and a farm is visible on the far side of the valley. The path now begins its descent and then bears right and left. Below you to the right another track will appear and above you to the left, Ebworth House. The path curves to the right here, after which you will be confronted by another choice – on the right, is a little trail linking the path with the track below; and, left, a path leading up to the ridge, which you take. This short but steep rise will bring you on to a farm track with a field ahead of you and the house to the left.

Turn left and head for the house. Pass through the farmyard, noting an interesting outhouse with unusual arches. Head directly for a gate set in a stone wall in front of you, passing on the left a stone building with a corrugated roof. Then aim for a wooden gate you see ahead of you. The gate will leave you on another track with a grid and stone gate pillars on the left. Ignore this and continue forward into a field with a stone wall – almost immediately you will see a stile in a corner made by the wall and some fir trees. Go through this into a narrow defile with the trees right and wall left. Soon you will come to another stile which will bring you into a field and bleaker open country. You need to cross this field diagonally to the right aiming for a solitary clump of trees in the middle which marks a spring. Pass just to the left of this until you see a gate in the hedge on the other side of the field. To the right of this you will see a large stile in the corner (not to be confused with another gate and track further to the right). Cross the stile and walk forward, at the same angle as the stile, towards a gap in the hedge, next to a solitary tree. To your right is Overtown, a group of buildings including an older, handsome edifice of uncertain origin.

Pass through the gap into another field, heading for another tree on its own, perhaps marked with a yellow arrow. Beyond you will see another lone tree, rather eccentric in appearance, and beyond that the fields roll down to woodland and the buildings of Brook Farm. However, make a sharp turn right, between a house, right, and the eccentric tree, left, and walk down towards the wood. A stream is splashing down the hill with you – cross it as soon as you can and continue down, past a wheezing pump dressed in brick, to a gate at the edge of the wood.

Behind you the stream looks quite impressive as it leaps down the hillside; but go through the gate and enter the wood on a wide path flanked by spindly trees. This will soon bring you back onto Cranham Common and as you walk forward, with Painswick visible to the southwest, you will recognise the houses and school from where you started.

Cranham

The poet and playwright James Elroy Flecker spent several months in a sanatorium here in 1910.

Sheepscombe

Sheepscombe features a great deal in Laurie Lee's classic 'Cider with Rosie'.

The CRANHAM - SHEEPSCOMBE Walk

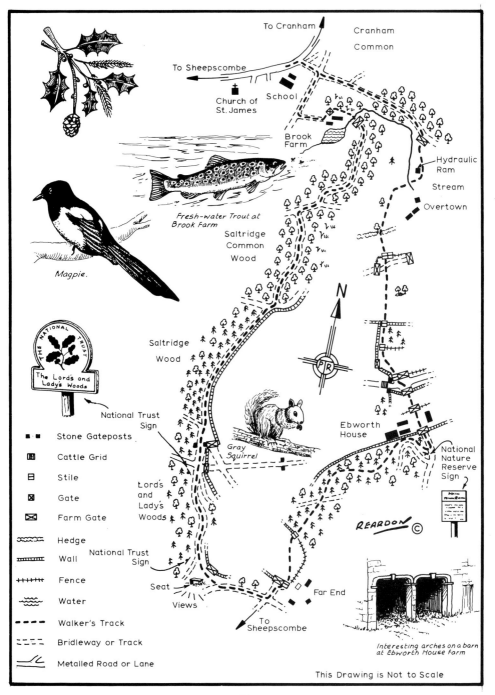

To Cranham

Cranham Common

To Sheepscombe

Church of St. James

School

Brook Farm

Hydraulic Ram

Stream

Overtown

Fresh-water Trout at Brook Farm

Saltridge Common Wood

Magpie.

N

P R

Saltridge Wood

The Lords and Lady's Woods

National Trust Sign

Gray Squirrel

Ebworth House

National Nature Reserve Sign

Lord's and Lady's Woods

National Trust Sign

REARDON ©

Seat

Far End

Views

To Sheepscombe

▪-▪	Stone Gateposts
	Cattle Grid
⊟	Stile
⊠	Gate
⊠	Farm Gate
∿∿∿	Hedge
⊞⊞⊞	Wall
+++++	Fence
∿∿	Water
- - -	Walker's Track
⌐⌐⌐	Bridleway or Track
⌒	Metalled Road or Lane

Interesting arches on a barn at Ebworth House farm

This Drawing is Not to Scale

11

3. Minchinhampton Common

Distance: 4 miles
Time: Under 2 hours of continuous walking
Map: OS Pathfinder SO 80/90 (Stroud)
Starting point: grid reference 873008. Centre of Minchinhampton.
Terrain: grassy common for the most part. A little track and some metalled surface on back lanes. Mud is a possibility but the height and open nature of Minchinhampton common means the ground is usually dry.
Refreshments: Several inns in Minchinhampton, including the 18th century Crown Hotel. En route is the Old Lodge Inn.

THIS walk is bracing yet it involves almost no climbing and is effortlessly refreshing. There is plenty of grass to be trod on Minchinhampton Common but the altitude (about 650ft) should mean that mud is only a minor hindrance, allowing you to take in the panorama of the Frome and Nailsworth valleys.

Park where you are able in Minchinhampton, but preferably in the vicinity of the Holy Trinity Church, with its distinctive spire. Minchinhampton is a surprisingly attractive small town, with narrow streets, houses in local stone and a lovely market square, with its pillared Market Hall of the seventeenth century, and Queen Anne post office. Minchinhampton grew up as a cloth town and was also an important producer of oolitic limestone. However, during the nineteenth century the focus of business shifted to the new factories in the Stroud Valley below. The church with its 'truncated steeple trimmed with pinnacles', has a brass commemorating James Bradley, Astronomer-Royal in 1742, who was the discoverer of the aberration of fixed stars. The church is also notable for the vaulting beneath the tower and its beautiful south transept, built in 1382 by Robert de la Bere, whose effigy is beneath the south window.

The church is in Bell Lane and is blessed with public lavatories opposite. Pass the church on your right, bear right around the wall into a lane lined with cropped trees and to their left a school playground, and head for the common that you see before you.

Minchinhampton Common, in part a golf course, is about six hundred acres of conserved land, the largest such expanse south of Cleeve and was used for grazing livestock as far back as Norman times.

When you reach the common, turn left along the path marked 'Private Road', with the stone wall on the left and follow the subtly rising slope. As you continue along, some attractive houses appear beyond the wall to the left. After a short while the path will peter out and land you on the grass. The wall, however, remains always on the left. The main road, meanwhile, is not very far distant to the right.

Very soon you will come to a mound. A sunken lane, which feeds the main road, appears immediately after. Cross over this, the wall still to the left, modern houses beyond it for the most part now, and forge ahead. The road on the right nips in ever closer but whilst you do not need to hug the wall on the left, keep it in mind, for the

The Market Square
MINCHINHAMPTON

REARDON

true path is not entirely clear. The wall turns fairly sharply leftwards and is no longer of naturally shaped boulders, but hewn blocks. By now the common is quite flat and has become a golf course. To the right views begin to open up to a distant ridge and the hollow of a deep valley before it. On the left you will pass a set of gates which lead to a house with a turret.

Then you will soon pass, on the left, another set of wrought-iron gates, this time with gold flourishes. Then the wall comes to an end revealing an open expanse of grass to the left and the stark lines of rugby posts in the distance. Ahead of you amid some trees and behind a wall are some houses - you should head for the right hand corner of the wall.

The mounds that you will see in this area of the common - you may have followed the rather tempting ridge of one on the approach to the end of the wall - are called the Bulwarks. These are the remains of the largest Iron Age hillfort in this part of England. It is thought that it was here that the last Iron Age tribesmen, retreating northwards, made a final stand against the advancing Romans and were routed.

In making for the corner of the wall you will cross a road. Continue forward with the wall on your left and as it swings away to the left follow the gaps in the Bulwarks ahead of you, or perhaps slightly to the right, and make for the road and a house you can see beyond it, the Old Lodge Inn. On the other side of the road you will see a lane, marked by a signpost with the name of the Inn, leading straight to the Inn in question.

Follow the lane as far as the pub. Before you are views across the valley to the hills and skyline beyond, as well as a crowd of modern and not very prepossessing houses. The lane bears around to the left but you should turn sharp right here and set out across the golf course in the general direction of the houses of Amberley that you will see beyond a road on the other side of the common.

As you proceed the view into the valley on the left becomes ever deeper, whilst there is little to be seen on the right except for a fenced mound the other side of the road that may be a reservoir. Cross the road carefully (it is busier than might be expected), thread your way through the mounds and continue to head for the houses, aiming to land at their right flank, by the war memorial that will become visible as you proceed forward. On the left a sudden hollow will appear and below it a row of chimneys. As you approach Amberley look below, to the left of the leftermost house of the village, to a large chapel in the valley.

13

Make your way across a road to the war memorial, from where there are more fine views across the valleys. Along a street to the left there is a row of cottages built cheek by jowl with satisfying picturesqueness.

Amberley has a notable, if unfashionable, literary association. 'John Halifax, Gentleman', written by Mrs Craik in 1857 is a true Victorian story of perseverance in the face of adversity that would have warmed the heart of Mrs Thatcher. John Halifax is a young man of ability who is adopted by a mill owning family and who eventually takes over the business. Needless to say his path to the top is far from easy but, sure enough, he overcomes the obstacles he meets and at the end he enjoys peace of mind and of heart, though the book ends with his death. The style is a little prim and sentimental but no less enjoyable, as a period piece, for that. Much of the book was written while Mrs Craik was in residence at Rose Cottage - Enderley is Amberley and Enderley Flat is the Common.

From the war memorial turn back to recross the road towards a large house. Keep to its right, passing a little shelter crowned with a weather vane, and walk alongside the stone wall which will be on your left. The wall soon turns sharply left but you should continue walking onwards across the common until you meet a road. The ground rises slightly here and you will probably hear the sound of traffic ahead. On your right you will see the mound of the reservoir.

As you approach the road you will see a cluster of trees on the other side, surrounded by a low stone wall. Aim for this. Immediately before the road there is a series of dips and hollows that may be inconvenient to clamber across - in this case you can skirt around them to the left.

Cross the road and walk to the right. You will notice that the road you have just crossed soon meets a crossroads and that a road leads down left from the crossroads to the houses of Burleigh. So bear diagonally left across the common, crossing a track in the process, down towards the point where the road enters the village. Ignore the road, marked with a 'No Through Road' sign, that climbs up around the back of the village but descend into the village, passing the 30 mph signs, until you come to a proper red telephone box.

Pass the telephone box and the bus stop and turn right into the narrow road which appears after the next house. This lane passes West Lodge on the left and then narrows to enter a sort of gully with a high wall to the right which bears a distinctly fortified look. As you leave this mighty rampart behind, a low, stone wall, offering fine views to the Golden Valley, will appear to the left.

The lane rises a little - the nearest thing to a climb that you will meet during the whole walk - and passes Cherry Tree Cottage on the right. Then you come to a junction, where a handsome period house overlooks the valley. Bear left, pass the house (Burleigh House) on your right and then bear almost immediately right at the next junction. These twin junctions that come so quickly one after the other are called the Roundabouts. The lane threads its way through a succession of cottages and houses and then comes to another junction where you should turn right.

Continue straight on until very soon you come to a larger road. Cross this to find yourself back on the common and before you the singular view of Minchinhampton Church. Head across the common towards it until you come to the lane on the right which runs down to Bell Lane and the town centre.

The MINCHINHAMPTON Walk

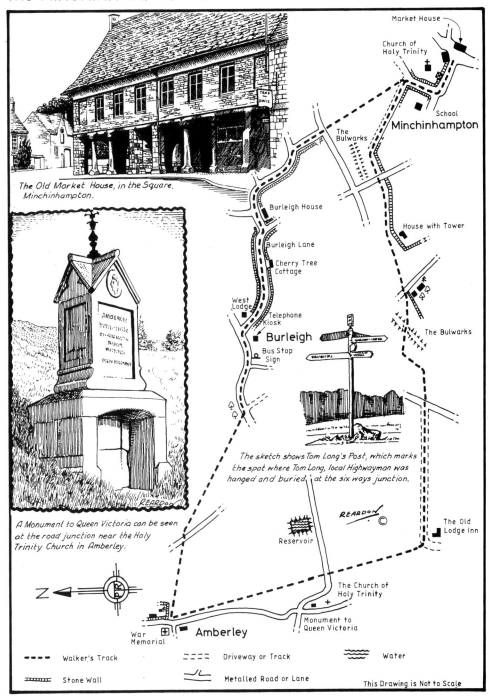

The Old Market House, in the Square, Minchinhampton.

Market House

Church of Holy Trinity

School

Minchinhampton

The Bulwarks

Burleigh House

House with Tower

Burleigh Lane

Cherry Tree Cottage

West Lodge

Telephone Kiosk

Burleigh

The Bulwarks

Bus Stop Sign

The sketch shows Tom Long's Post, which marks the spot where Tom Long, local Highwayman was hanged and buried, at the six ways junction.

AMBERLEY

A Monument to Queen Victoria can be seen at the road junction near the Holy Trinity Church in Amberley.

REARDON ©

Reservoir

The Old Lodge Inn

The Church of Holy Trinity

Monument to Queen Victoria

War Memorial

Amberley

- - - -   Walker's Track   = = = =   Driveway or Track   ～～～   Water

🚃🚃🚃   Stone Wall   ⌐⌐⌐   Metalled Road or Lane   This Drawing is Not to Scale

15

4. Eastleach Martin/Eastleach Turville

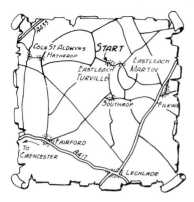

Distance: 4¼ miles
Time: max 2/2½ hours
Map: In the OS Pathfinder series the route crosses from one (SP 00/10) to another (SP 20/30). Otherwise the route is clear enough from the OS Landranger 163.
Starting Point: Grid Ref: 202053
Terrain: mostly track and field with a little road. On the whole the going is easy, mostly level with a couple of brief ascents.
Refreshments: The Victoria Pub in Eastleach Turville is a very pleasant old inn. Otherwise nearby Fairford offers several pubs and cafes.

THE following walk starts from the twin villages of Eastleach Martin and Eastleach Turville which lie close to the border with Oxfordshire, a little way northeast of Fairford. The combined villages produce a hybrid that is among the most charming in the Cotswolds. The walk allows you to visit their two churches, separated by the River Leach and an ancient bridge; and takes you across field, through woodland and along a Roman road.

Park carefully off the road in or near the village. In the western part of the village above the main street you will see the Victoria Inn and opposite, a row of cottages with a distinctive clock tower. Walk eastwards and down towards the river on the Burford road passing a number of 19th century cottages. Soon you will find yourself at a junction near the river, with the road curving away, left, towards the churches. To your left, a memorial cross; to your right, a cluster of well preserved buildings, including a gorgeous entrance to Troutbeck Farm (private), and a proper telephone box. The whole of this scene warrants a moment's contemplation - it is extraordinarily pretty, whether on a simmering summer's day, or in the misty, blue chill of winter. No chocolate-box village this, just one that carries on as it always has, exuding a rural calm.

Proceed along the stone path, through a forest of daffodils in Spring, by the river towards the church. Very quickly you will come to a rare and ancient clapper bridge, or Keble's Bridge as it is known locally, consisting of a series of rock slabs resting on low pillars. Bridges of this type were not constructed until the 18th century. Walk across this one over the limpid River Leach from Eastleach Turville to Eastleach Martin, bear left onto the stone path and follow this into the churchyard. Once again there are pretty views across the river.

The church of St. Michael and St. Martin, Eastleach Martin, became redundant in 1982, whilst the church of Eastleach Turville, visible across the river, remains open for communal worship. Nonetheless, this church, in the hands of the Redundant Churches Fund, is in a fine state of repair and may be visited. That two small villages should lie adjacent, each with its own church, may seem unusual. The probable explanation, however, is that the land was once owned by two different lords. An old name for Eastleach Martin is Bouthrop, also the name of a nearby farm. The church was originally Norman though many changes were made in the 13th century. Worthy of note are the expressive carved hands in the north transept and the 17th century chest in the chancel.

Continue through the churchyard with the church on your left and exit by the gate to the road and turn left until you quickly arrive at a triangular junction. Turn right and take the lower road in the direction of Holwell. After about 150 yards you will pass a house behind a wall, right, with the river meandering to your left beneath a file of graceful trees. The road takes you past a stone wall, left, and the remains of a stone building. Soon the river veers away as you emerge in more open country, with a wind pump appearing ahead of you to the left.

A gate and track, which you ignore, lead away to the left. Remain on this quiet road for another 100 yards or so, where the road begins to rise rather steeply. Here, on your left, you will see another gate. Take this onto a clear farm track and keep to it as it follows a line of trees to its left. The village is now invisible and the track is at the bottom of a field steeply banked like an early motor race-track. Before you, fields interlock away to the horizon. The track pierces a line of berried trees right and the remains of a stone wall, left, and soon forks. Take the right, upper path, to the right of a large tree, after which it curves to the right around the girth of the slope which is alive with rabbit and hare.

Soon woodland, Sheephouse Plantation, will appear in front of you. Head for this, noticing the curious ribbed pattern on the field beside you. Whether this is all that remains of ancient ploughing practices, or merely paths trod by generations of sheep, is hard to tell. When you reach the corner of the wood, turn left with a stone wall and the wood, filled with flapping pigeons, to your right. Soon the wood ends at a gated field. Ignore it and walk on, with the field to your right. At your back is a clear view of the lines scored regularly across the face of the slope where you were walking a few minutes before. Follow the curve of the walled field until you reach a sort of logged fence in the corner. Hop over this to find yourself on an unlikely looking path, all but invisible, at the bottom margin of the sloping, cultivated field, right. Walk on, with the barbed wire fence to your left, taking care to avoid treading the crop. At the end of the field you will find a gate which you pass into a pasture meadow with woodland at its far end.

Stay on the left hand margin, with the field sloping up to the right, and aim for a bridge ahead of you, left. Cross the fence into the next pasture by means of this corral like bridge across the Leach (though staying on the same bank of the river) and aim for a small gate you see before you leading into Smeril Plantation. A short way up the slope, right, you will pass a solitary enclosed tree shading a little wooden headstone that commemorates the death of one 'Misty'.

The Church at Eastleach Martin.

17

As you approach the gate you will notice a small area of lush marshland over the fence to the left, presumably made thus by springs. Enter the wood by the gate and follow a vague path ahead of you keeping pretty well to the left margin which looks out onto open fields. Occasionally the path slips a little further into the wood and then returns to the edge, before, after no more than 300 yards, it enters definitively as an old stone wall, and a ditch (actually the river) sheer off below to the left. At this point, in a small messy clearing, the path is vaguer than ever but follow your nose a short way up the slope through the trees to the right which will bring you out of the wood over a broken wall onto the edge of a field.

Turn left and follow the margin of the field with the impenetrable looking woodland on your left. The boundary describes a 'U' here, taking you down a bit, along the bottom then up the other side until you are standing pretty well opposite your exit point from the wood. Continue along the margin, left, with the wood still alongside you, ignoring a gap in a section of broken wall at one corner after about 300 yards. A short way after this, perhaps 150 yards, the track passes through a stone wall and bears left still following the contour of the wood, left. The track dips down to a track which you take as it re-enters the wood on the left. This is what remains of Akeman Street, the Roman Road that linked Cirencester with Bicester and St. Albans and one of the few whose route has not been retained as part of the main road network.

Follow what is now a muddy track through the wood until it rises up into an open field. Walk straight on beside a stone wall which is on the left margin of this field with fields sloping away beyond it and level, fertile land to your right. You are heading for a road some half a mile in front of you, invisible except for the occasional vehicle passing along it. Eventually you will see the road down ahead of you to the left, passing over pretty Sheep Bridge. At the road turn left towards the bridge, passing on the right a cattle grid and track running between green amphitheatrical slopes. Cross the bridge and just short of a road junction turn left through a gate into a field.

Cross the field diagonally, following a clearly incised path along the valley bottom until it meets the far slope which you then follow as it curves left, and sharply right. You will now find yourself opposite the wood you were in earlier. Keep close to the slope, right, with the wood across to the left and walk on towards a gate which leads to the right of the marshy field seen earlier. You then come to another gate which leads past the corral bridge and into a defile that opens into another field. Follow its right margin to another gate in the top right corner, as the field makes a gradual ascent. At the top you will have your most complete view of the area and the route you have taken. You are close to home now and you need only continue through gates in the same direction until you see the buildings that mark the edge of Eastleach. Beside a red farm building in the middle of the last field you will see a gate leading into the farmyard and on to the road where you turn right. Follow the road past several cottages until another junction with, behind you, a beautiful cottage smothered in creepers and shrubs. Turn left onto the road that leads below the Victoria Inn towards the heart of the village and the two churches.

Historical Note

One of England's great sons, John Keble, a founder member of the Oxford Movement and of Keble College, Oxford, was curate of Eastleach Martin between 1815 and 1825. He wrote many hymns and is particularly remembered for The Christian Year, a volume of sacred verse.

The EASTLEACH MARTIN/EASTLEACH TURVILLE Walk

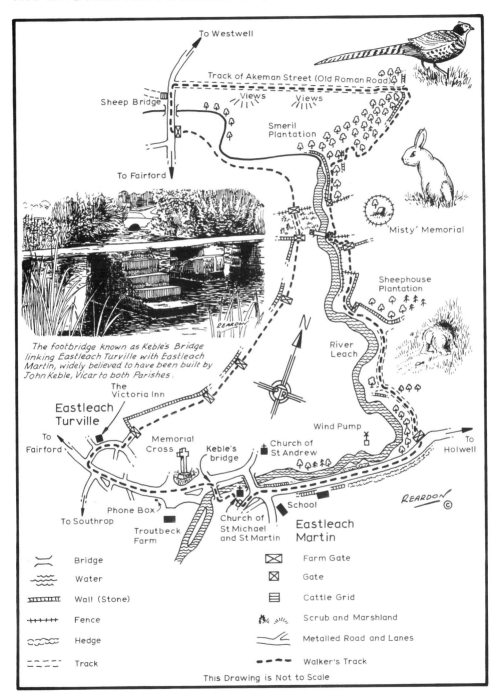

To Westwell

Track of Akeman Street (Old Roman Road)

Sheep Bridge

Views   Views

To Fairford

Smeril
Plantation

'Misty' Memorial

Sheephouse
Plantation

River
Leach

The footbridge known as Keble's Bridge
linking Eastleach Turville with Eastleach
Martin, widely believed to have been built by
John Keble, Vicar to both Parishes.

The
Victoria Inn

Eastleach
Turville

To
Fairford

Memorial
Cross

Keble's
bridge

Church of
St Andrew

Wind Pump

To
Holwell

Phone Box

To Southrop

Troutbeck
Farm

Church of
St Michael
and St Martin

School

Eastleach
Martin

REARDON ©

Symbol	Meaning	Symbol	Meaning
≋	Bridge	⊠	Farm Gate
∿	Water	⊠	Gate
▥	Wall (Stone)	▤	Cattle Grid
+++++	Fence		Scrub and Marshland
⌒⌒⌒	Hedge	⌇	Metalled Road and Lanes
- - - -	Track	▬ ▬ ▬	Walker's Track

This Drawing is Not to Scale

19

5. Guiting Power

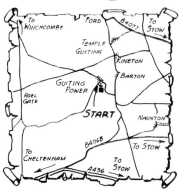

Distance: 4.5 miles
Time: 2/2.5 hours of uninterrupted walking
Map: OS Pathfinder SP 02/12 (Stow)
Starting point: grid reference 094248
Terrain: mostly track and paved surfaces with a little woodland path. A great deal of rain would be necessary to render this walk uncomfortable. It is an undulating route of sweet ascents and gentle slopes.
Refreshments: Two pubs in Guiting Power, Ye Olde Ine and the Farmers Arms. Alternatively, there is the Half Way House in Kineton.

THIS walk begins in the flourishing village of Guiting Power which lies to the east of Cheltenham and a little to the southeast of Winchcombe. It takes you along high ground across generally open countryside, with broad, majestic views. There is one foray into woodland. This is a walk for a crisp winter's day — the going firm and the colours burnished by pale sunlight.

You should be able to park in the centre of Guiting Power, just opposite the green and close to the post office. Guiting, apparently, is an old word meaning 'torrent'. The green, with its water pump and memorial to the local people who died in the First World War, is surrounded by solid, ancient houses in local stone, sitting about the green in artless harmony. All is neat, all is in order. Apart from the post office, the green also offers the inviting looking Guiting Guest House and a bakery and grocery shop.

Before setting out, you may care to have a look at St. Michael's Church, along the road leading away from the green. It sits in a pretty graveyard, behind which is a field with a couple of attractive barns. The church itself was built in the Norman period from which time the fine south doorway remains. The Chancel, in Early English style, dates from the 12th and 13th centuries. The tower is a 15th century addition. The congregation increased substantially in the 19th century and the church was enlarged accordingly; but by the end of the century a depressed economy saw the church in virtual ruin. It was saved by determined local effort to find the money for its restoration. The interior is attractive; but one of its curiosities is the tiny stone sarcophagus at the foot of the pulpit.

To start the walk, go left from the post office as you look at it towards the arched window of the distant Baptist Church, and then, almost immediately, take the first road on the right opposite a cottage raised on a bank. This road is signposted as a No Through Road. Now you notice that Guiting is fairly high up - to the right, beyond the vegetable plots, is a steep sided valley. The road threads its way quietly through a series of cottages, dips, rises past an old hay loft on the left with a blue door and comes to an end at a metal gate. On a chill, still winter morning the air is fragrant with smoke from hearth fires.

Go through the gate onto a grassy path where a field falls steeply away to the right into a gully along which a branch of the Windrush flows, beyond which trees, in a regular line, stand straight and prim. The path descends, enters a bushy defile and into woodland and then flattens out, briefly, and meets the rushing stream. Ahead of you the path begins to climb again; but you should turn right and cross a miniature arched stone bridge that spans the stream. The path then begins to climb up the other side, passing a small stone alcove built into the slope, once used, presumably, for storage.

The path rises gently enough through the trees, sweeping you away from the stream below. Then you will meet a bridle gate and passing through it will bring you into a sort of corral with wooden fencing on either side and a handsome farm house ahead. Below you to the left you can still hear the stream and see a large pond or small lake. Beyond is Guiting Wood.

Continue towards Castlett Farm. As you approach you will see notices asking you to ensure that your dog is on a lead because of the presence of livestock; and you will then, at the corner of the house, come to a crossroads, with cottages ahead of you. Turn left and walk through the farm with the house and farmyard to the left. You will pass a beautifully preserved barn, left, with wooden doors, before arriving at two stone gateposts and a paved track with a cottage on the other side.

Church of St Michael. Guiting Power.

Turn left here. Ahead of you is woodland, Guiting Wood again, and a sturdy manor house about two thirds of the way up the hill. Continue along the track until you come to the road, Critchford Lane, noticing on the left the stone slab announcing the entrance to Castlett Farm. Turn right and follow the road as it climbs between a clipped hedge to the right and a tall, wild hedgerow to the left. The hedges give way to open country. Behind you are good views of the vale. The road bumps over the crest and begins to descend - the rooftops of Kineton loom up from the valley in front of you. Continue down towards them, with a Passing Place sign on the left until you meet, about 200 yards from the village, a track on the left heralded by a sign warning that it is unsuitable for motors. Turn left onto this track. If, however, you are in need of refreshment there is a pub, the Half Way House, in Kineton, a village in which the Windrush is forded twice and which lies some 3 miles from the river's source.

The track heads towards woodland and ascends very slightly. As it begins to flatten out, turn to admire the views behind you. The fields slope gently away back towards Castlett Farm and beyond it rise up on a scale that somehow seems disproportionately large. Keep to the track, passing through a little tunnel of thicket into open country as the track begins its descent towards Sheephouse barn, with two arches, in front on the left, and chestnut coloured Guiting Wood beyond. Shortly after passing the barn you come to a crossroads and a paved road. The wide track on the left is guarded by three boulders one of which is unmistakably a giant, fearsome frog. Continue straight ahead on the paved road down towards the wood. You will hear the stream, which you cross, noticing the stone slab across it to the right, and turn immediately left along a track into the wood.

Guiting Wood borders the valley of the Castlett stream which bubbles away to the left of this paved track. The track rises imperceptibly until you notice that the stream is far beneath you; descends as the water gathers into a still pool in a clearing to the left where heron paddle sulkily; and then rises again. When it levels out again there is a field on a steep slope to the right and soon the branches of the trees on each side meet to form a tunnel and a patch of green beyond announces the end of the wood.

You emerge onto common-like ground with a cottage on the right and above it the manor house which has been visible much of the walk since leaving Castlett Farm. Follow the track towards a barn which sits to the left of some trees. You will come to a crossroads. Cross and head straight down towards a gate, ignoring the other track on the left that leads into a sort of paddock. Go through the gate and follow the track. After a few hundred yards Castlett Farm will appear on the left and then another farm in front of you. When you reach this farm, at a junction where a track rises to the right, turn left towards a large barn and take the path that plunges down into woodland towards the sound of the stream. Keep the stream to the left and as the path bottoms out you will realise that you have been here before, for a path on the left meets the little stone bridge you crossed earlier. So, ignore the bridge and walk straight ahead, up out of the woods and back into Guiting Power.

The GUITING POWER Walk

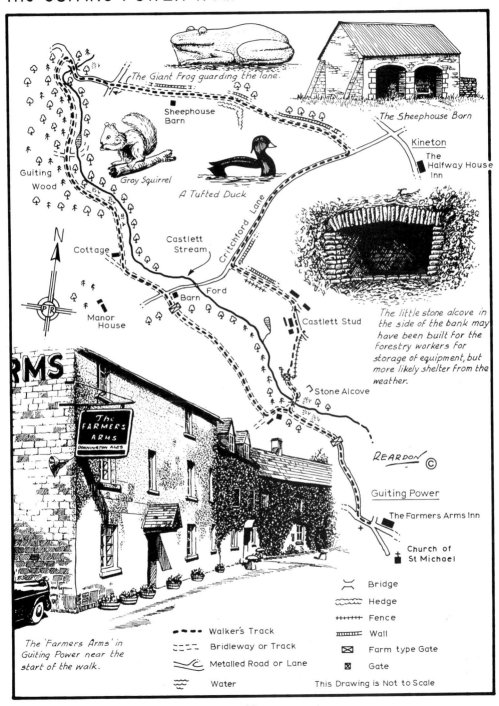

The Giant Frog guarding the lane.

Sheephouse Barn

The Sheephouse Barn

Kineton

The Halfway House Inn

Gray Squirrel

Guiting Wood

A Tufted Duck

Castlett Stream

Critchford Lane

Cottage

N

P R

Manor House

Barn   Ford

Castlett Stud

The little stone alcove in the side of the bank may have been built for the forestry workers for storage of equipment, but more likely shelter from the weather.

Stone Alcove

RMS

The FARMERS ARMS
DONNINGTON ALES

REARDON ©

Guiting Power

The Farmers Arms Inn

Church of St Michael

	Bridge
	Hedge
	Fence
	Wall
•- - - Walker's Track	⊠ Farm type Gate
- - - - Bridleway or Track	⊠ Gate
Metalled Road or Lane	
Water	This Drawing is Not to Scale

The 'Farmers Arms' in Guiting Power near the start of the walk.

6. Broadway/Laverton/Buckland

Distance: 4.5 miles
Time: 2.5 hours of uninterrupted walking,
Map: OS Pathfinder SP 03/13
Starting point: grid ref 094375
Terrain: the route takes you across fields, through woodland and along sunken paths, all of which are quite likely to be very muddy. There are a couple of stiff slopes to deal with, though nothing impossibly testing. You will pass through the two attractive villages of Laverton and Buckland.
Refreshments: Many inns and tea rooms in Broadway.

THIS walk begins and ends in one of the most famous of Cotswold towns, Broadway. Its fame, which rests on the superb array of ancient and beautifully preserved houses, manors and cottages that line its streets, draws thousands of visitors, particularly in summer. A walk in late winter or early spring will avoid the crowds.

You should have little trouble in finding a parking place off the road along the main street of Broadway. The walk begins by walking along the Snowshill road which runs south from Broadway at the west end of the town by the War Memorial and opposite the Swan Hotel.

Before you leave (or when you return), you may care to take a stroll along the wide street that is the backbone of the town. Almost every building is of some charm and in the Lygon Arms, with its fine restaurant, you have one of the most celebrated hotels in the country. Most of the stone houses date back to the 17th and 18th centuries.

Start walking along the Snowshill Road passing the Crown and Trumpet Inn on the left and some very handsome houses on the other side of the road. Continue past the Victorian church on the left until, on the right, you will notice a signposted lane which you take. Broadway's older church, St. Eadburgha's, is about three-quarters of a mile further along the Snowshill road - originally of Norman construction it boasts a most attractive interior.

Follow the lane, with cottages on the right, down to a kissing gate on the edge of a field. Go into the field and head for a stile and a bridge ahead of you which spans a stream cut deeply into the field. Beyond, you see fields leading up to woodland. Behind you, as you approach the bridge, the Cotswold edge hangs over the town and at its summit you cannot help but notice the cream castellations of Broadway Tower, a Gothic folly built by the Earl of Coventry in 1800. From its battlements at 1023 feet above sea level it is said to be possible to look into fourteen counties. Between 1822 and 1862 it housed the private printing press of Sir Thomas Philipps; later the poet William Morris, leader of the Oxford Movement, stayed here with the Pre-Raphaelite painter Burne-Jones and the poet Dante Gabriel Rossetti. It is a landmark that will be visible to you for a large part of this walk.

Having crossed the bridge there is an obvious track leading away before you to a gate in the corner of the field to the right of a red brick cottage with severely sloping roof. Go through the gate onto a minor road, cross it and enter the path on the other side of the road, practically opposite. This takes you into a defile between a hedge and a fence. Follow this as it climbs upwards, kinks to the right and then to the left and finally deposits you by means of a stile into a sloping field, with a paddock and house on the left and woodland, Broadway Coppice, at the top of the field. You are to head up the field, following a left diagonal course along a faintly visible path until you come to a gate into the wood set into the top left hand corner. As you puff your way up you may be grateful to pause to look at Broadway spread out behind you. Once in the wood follow the obvious path, which climbs still, and meets a junction of paths after some fifty yards where you bear left. The path soon swings right, up, then left to a gate at the edge of a field.

Follow the clear left margin of this field. As you continue the slope on the other side of the valley becomes visible ahead of you with coarse looking pasture and scrubby patches of hedge and woodland; whilst to the left Broadway Tower continues to stand out like a sentinel beacon. Pass a bridle gate on the left, after which the countryside opens up to the left and the path descends towards a white metal gate, where, to its right, a cream cottage sits in the hollow of a narrow valley. Hop over the stile next to the gate and head towards a farm building, a stable perhaps, which you keep to the right as you continue forward either by means of stiles or through an open gate. After about one hundred yards you come to another metal white gate on the right. Go through that by means of a stile, with the stable on the right, until after a few yards you meet a farm track where you turn left. This firm, straight track runs between two wooden fences and ascends gently towards woodland. On the left, across the valley, is Broadway Tower whilst to the right are distant hills. After about two hundred and fifty yards you'll pass a large barn on the right and then pass through a gateway as the track rises a little more steeply towards some farm buildings. Just before these farm buildings is a gate with a cluster of stiles to its left. Cross the first stile on to a path and then take another stile immediately to the right, which will bring you into the farmyard. Look left to face Buckland Wood and bear immediately right with hedge on the right and a gate before you (there is likely to be a signpost for the Cotswold Way).

You climb the gate and find yourself in a field which may well be filled with livestock and horses - dogs will most certainly need to be on a lead here. Follow the margin of the field as it bears left, with woodland above you to the left, and then right to another gate. Pass through this gate into another field, keeping to the track on the right hand margin of the field and passing the stump of an old stone gatepost. Ignore a stile you will pass on the right but not the fine views beyond it across the vale and Broadway Tower still at your back. Continue along this muddy track towards a gate you will see ahead of you. Go through the gate to a track near some trees that will deliver you at a crossroads just to the right of another gate.

The Cotswold Way continues forward but you should take the bridle path immediately on the right as it descends through a gate towards Laverton. This path is like a furrow cut deep into the hillside and takes you comfortably and obviously, if muddily, all the way down, with good views to the right. Eventually, where the land opens up a little, you will pass through a metal gate. Laverton soon becomes visible at the base of the hill and although the path is fairly clear, if you are in any doubt, the village is your destination. At the bottom the path meets a stream on the left and a wooden gate by the spectre of a tall, lifeless tree stump. Pass through the gate into the quiet village of Laverton and walk straight ahead until you see the Post Office on the right and, opposite the old school house, with its bell tower on the roof, a path on your right between stone walls leading to Buckland.

The path is clear and will after some minutes lead you past some cottages on the left to a road at the entrance to the tranquil village of Buckland, the church of which has 15th century glass and a painted panel said to have come from Hailes Abbey. Buckland Manor, now a luxury hotel, is mentioned by the 18th century writer, Mrs Delaney, in her 'Autobiography'. In 1715 she was to head to the manor which she was pleased to call The Farm, from London where her uncle, Lord Landsdowne, was in the Tower for his Jacobite sympathies. Efforts were made by government officers to prevent her and her family making the five day journey to Buckland - there was fainting and hysterics and only the arrival of her formidable aunt allowed them to leave the capital.

Turn right towards the village and proper red telephone box after which on the left is the entrance to a nursery and then a turning, also on the left, along a narrow lane with pretty, summery cottages on the left and the handsome 15th century rectory on the right, once visited by John Wesley but now 'developed'.

The lane abruptly narrows to a little footbridge across a stream and a gate which you pass through. Some fifty yards beyond is a stile which takes you into a field. The path slopes upward towards the woods of Burhill and another stile into another field and then yet another stile. Once you have crossed this third stile head up to a pair of oak trees and then towards some bushes. Whilst you are indeed nearing the wood, the path is in fact taking you around it and providing excellent views to the left. The path will eventually bring you to another stile and into another field. Looking across the field, slightly to the right, you will notice a bridle gate leading into Broadway Coppice. So cross the field and go through the gate onto another muddy path (ignoring the path immediately to the right) which ascends through thicket. After a few hundred yards the path levels out and opens up to the left and looks down on to Broadway. Soon you will cross a stile and then re-enter the wood at a junction of paths where you keep left. Follow the main path until you come to another stile at the edge of the wood at the top of a field, with Broadway below you. Cross the stile and strike immediately left, hugging the left margin of the field as you descend towards a stile that will bring you onto a farm track that leads to the road. Turn right and after about 150 yards you will see on the left the entrance to the field along which you retrace your steps, crossing the stream and heading for the church, to Broadway.

The BROADWAY/LAVERTON/BUCKLAND Walk

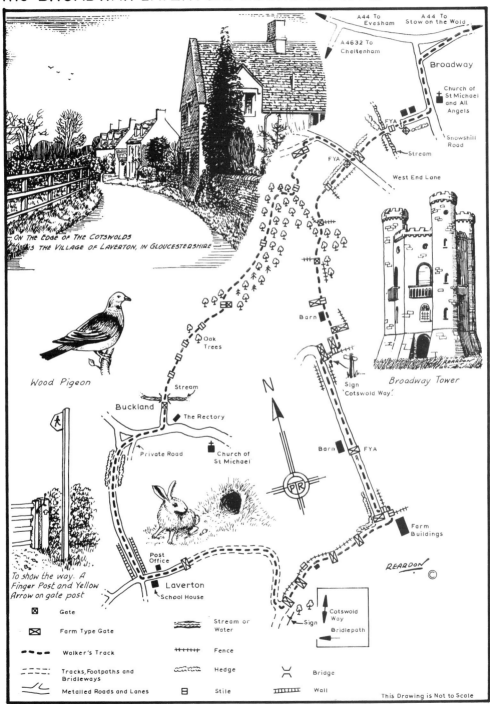

A44 To Evesham
A44 To Stow on the Wold
A4632 To Cheltenham

Broadway

Church of St Michael and All Angels

FYA

Snowshill Road

Stream

FYA

West End Lane

ON THE EDGE OF THE COTSWOLDS IS THE VILLAGE OF LAVERTON, IN GLOUCESTERSHIRE

Barn

Broadway Tower

Oak Trees

Wood Pigeon

Stream

Sign 'Cotswold Way'

Buckland

The Rectory

N

Private Road

Church of St Michael

Barn

FYA

P/R

Farm Buildings

REARDON ©

Post Office

Laverton

School House

To show the way. A Finger Post and Yellow Arrow on gate post

Sign

Cotswold Way
Bridlepath

Gate

Farm Type Gate

Walker's Track

Tracks, Footpaths and Bridleways

Metalled Roads and Lanes

Stream or Water

Fence

Hedge

Stile

Bridge

Wall

This Drawing is Not to Scale

27

7. Pope's Wood

Distance: 4.5 miles
Time: 2/2.5 hours of continuous walking
Map: OS Pathfinder SO 81/91 (Gloucester)
Starting Point: Grid Reference: 879128.
Royal William Hotel on the A46 Cheltenham
to Painswick road.
Terrain: Mostly woodland paths with a little
field walking and a couple of short excursions
onto roads. Very little of this walk is flat.
Many of the paths may well be wet and
muddy if the weather has been inclement.
Refreshments: Royal William Hotel and the
Prinknash Abbey tea rooms

THIS walk is more arduous than some, with gradients of one sort or another being its principal characteristic. In compensation, it contains some fine views and much of the route passes through ancient beech forest which is particularly beautiful in autumn.

Y ou should have no problem in parking your car in the area of the Royal William, although the car park behind it is for the exclusive use of patrons. If you were emerging from the pub onto the A46 you would turn left in the direction of Cheltenham. You will notice that there is a path on the left hand side of the road and by following this you will arrive at a signpost for Cranham and Birdlip; but if you prefer to avoid walking in the company of traffic, you will notice after a few yards on the right, across the road, a track that disappears into the undergrowth. Take this - it is a good, solid path which leads you into the woods. Shortly, with some heartwarming views across the valley to the right, you will come to a metalled lane. Turn left here and then almost immediately right and continue along another path through the woods. You will cross another path - continue forward until you see another lane ahead of you, Mill Lane, which rises up to the A46 just about at the point that you want. Turn right onto the A46, pass Cranham Close with its stone wall, and then, almost at once, turn right again, towards Cranham and Birdlip, keeping to the left hand side of the road.

After some fifty yards you will pass a bungalow on the left and see a road on the right signposted for Cranham Scout HQ. Ignore this but turn, instead, into the woods on the left. A signpost explains that you are heading towards Cooper's Hill and Birdlip via the Cotswold Way. Another explains that you are entering Buckholt Wood which is part of the Cotswold Commons and Beechwoods National Nature Reserve and includes some of the best examples of ancient beechwood habitat in the Cotswolds. The area has been wooded for hundreds of years and contains many examples of ancient beechwood animals and plants. It is managed to produce timber using techniques that maintain intact its character and conservation value.

Enter the still of the wood, with a substantial stone wall on the left and thick, straggling woodland roundabout. The path here is a little narrower than the preceding ones and is already ascending slightly. Soon the wood opens up a little to become a glade, offering good views towards Gloucester and the Severn Valley. Ignore another path leading in from the right and just follow the path you are on up through the trees which begin to close in more as the path rises more steeply. Out of the undergrowth long trees with smooth reptilinear trunks rise skywards. The path curves slightly leftwards, still at a considerable gradient, hemmed in by saplings and boughs. Shortly thereafter is an easing of the gradient and we can begin to be optimistic that it is about to come to an end - the summit cannot be far. The wall reappears to the left and you come to a triangle and a meeting of paths.

At this point ignore the path coming in from the right and bear left and straight along the main path as it plunges downwards. You will pass a notice concerning Buckholt Wood on your right and the wall still present on your left. As the path falls away steeply, the woodland is more open and there is even a glimpse of fields to the right. You will pass a couple of grassy tracks which are to be ignored; the wall on the left wears a caparison of ivy and creeper and the path becomes even steeper. The vegetation on either side is dense. The path widens and firms up a little as yellow stone protrudes through the earth; and then as the path begins to level out it veers away to the right.

From the left the hum of traffic rises from the A46 beneath you. The path reaches another intersection and triangle from which sprouts a cluster of tall, spindly trees. Turn sharp left here and descend beneath a dark canopy of trees to the main road on what is really a track with wheel ruts either side of the crown. Then the track opens up to reveal extensive views to the plain and hills ahead of you, passes a cottage on the left and curls, right, to the road.

Cross the A46 with care, admire the splendid panorama and turn left to follow the narrow path to the bend in the road, with a meadow on your right. After about fifty yards, just by the chevrons, a little path drops down to the right and passes through a narrow halter-like stile into a field. The large ochre building with modern lines is Prinknash Abbey, which was established in 1928, when a Benedictine community moved here from Caldey Island.

Turn right and follow the right hand margin of the field, passing beneath a chestnut tree. You will find a stile in the corner next to a rusting wrought iron gate. Cross this and enter another field which descends past barbed wire on the right with the abbey on the left. Beyond to the left, a patrician-looking house with elegant garden sits at the foot of dense woodland. This is the 'old abbey', a grange built originally in the 14th century for the Abbots of Gloucester. Horace Walpole visited it in 1714 and wrote: 'It stands on a glorious but impracticable hill in the midst of a little forest of beech, and commanding Elysium.'

Ahead the land undulates and is for the most part pasture, dotted with sheep and cattle and thatched with patches of woodland. In the bottom right hand corner of the field you will meet an eccentric looking gate by an overgrown stile which you pass through into another field. Head down towards the large chestnut tree ahead of you. Cross the stile beside it and head to another chestnut tree, enjoying the view of the hills away to the distant right. Then aim for the dead tree in the middle - behind you Buckholt Wood stretches across the skyline whilst in front the field descends to a long hedge. Head down towards the bottom left corner, where rows of tall, feathery trees shimmer serenely above dense bush.

Cross the stile, then a footbridge, to keep precisely to the right of way, and bear left across the grass to a stile in a metal fence. Once on the track turn left and immediately right over another similar stile. Now you are in a field - keep to its left hand margin as it rises. As you approach a red brick house near the top you will see a stile on the left. Cross this into another field and turn right. Pass the house on the right and cross another stile into a lane. Turn left and walk its steepish gradient until you pass a private entrance to Prinknash on the left. Woodland appears to the right soon after, and a way into it, which you must ignore, for that is Kites Hill and is private; but a few yards beyond is the entrance to Pope's Wood. Turn right into it along a short stony path which joins a substantial track, pass the notice which explains that this too is ancient beechland and continue until after about one hundred yards you reach a large clearing and a bewildering array of tracks.

Ignore the track, unmarked, on the left and also the next one on the left marked Public Bridleway - take instead the track pretty well directly ahead which is also a bridleway. The path is wide, possibly muddy and continues through thick woodland. Keep going for a fair while, fifteen minutes perhaps, ignoring any other tracks that encroach on the main one, which ascends gently. Enjoy the dead quiet of the place which is not unlike tropical jungle in its dense vegetation, heavy moistness and silence broken by only the occasional squawk.

Near the top you meet a major junction, where you must turn right passing another notice about Pope's Wood, onto a level path that leads into a sweeter and more open area of woodland. This path is right at the edge of the wood, and there are fields beyond. The soil at first is dark and loamy, and soft and springy underfoot, before degenerating into patches of mud. Then the path firms up again as it descends into the open and towards the jaws of more woodland before becoming a hard track which passes the manicured hedge of a house on the left and rises up to the main road, at Castle End.

Unfortunately, you must now walk along this road for about three hundred yards until, on the right, you see through a gap in the trees a stone wall running down across fields towards a cottage. At this point on the left is a track on the left leading away from the road up towards a common. Take this as it rises, ignore all tracks to the right and left. A grassy bank will appear to the right and woodland to the left falls away to where you were walking earlier. Eventually you will pass a shed on the left, then a cottage, and eventually the sight of sky above you suggests the top and in fact you arrive on a golf course. Unless you wish to visit Painswick Beacon, which is a few hundred yards to the right, the highest point hereabouts and mentioned in the poem 'Oak and Olive' by James Elroy Flecker, bear left and keep to the left margin of the course, with woodland on your left. If you hear a loud persistent cry, it is likely to emanate from the cockatoo that belongs to one of the residents on the edge of the course. The path leaves the golf course to become a firm track, passes a substantial building on the right, Castle Lodge, passes an entrance to Pope's Wood on the left, before becoming metalled road, arriving finally at the Royal William Hotel where you started.

The POPE'S WOOD Walk

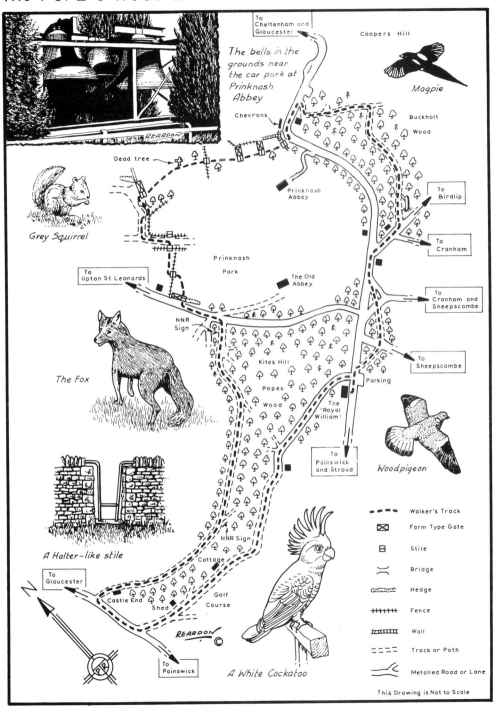

The bells in the grounds near the car park at Prinknash Abbey

Magpie

Grey Squirrel

The Fox

A Halter-like stile

A White Cockatoo

Woodpigeon

To Cheltenham and Gloucester

Coopers Hill

Buckholt Wood

Chevrons

Dead tree

Prinknash Abbey

To Birdlip

To Cranham

Prinknash Park

To Upton St Leonards

The Old Abbey

To Cranham and Sheepscombe

NNR Sign

To Sheepscombe

Kites Hill

Popes

Wood

Parking

The 'Royal William'

To Painswick and Stroud

NNR Sign

Cottage

To Gloucester

Castle End   Shed

Golf Course

REARDON ©

To Painswick

Legend:

- - -	Walker's Track
⊠	Farm Type Gate
⊟	Stile
⌣	Bridge
∞∞∞	Hedge
++++++	Fence
⊓⊓⊓⊓	Wall
====	Track or Path
⌇	Metalled Road or Lane

This Drawing is Not to Scale

N

8. Stanway/Stanton

Distance: 5 miles
Time: $2\frac{1}{2}$ hours of uninterrupted walking
Map: OS Pathfinder 1043 (SP 03/13), (Broadway and Chipping Campden)
Starting point: grid reference 062323
Terrain: a little road, a lot of field, a fair climb, some mud.
Getting there: Stanway House lies just north of the B4077, the Stow to Tewkesbury Road.
Refreshments: Mount Inn at Stanton

THIS walk is a little more challenging than some — but worth it. Challenging because of a substantial climb up Shenbarrow Hill but worth it because of two beautiful Cotswold villages and some magnificent views. If you do not wish to tackle the hill, it is still possible to enjoy views and villages by merely walking to Stanton and back the same way.

Park well off the road in the vicinity of Stanway House. Before you commence the walk, take time to gaze upon one of the fairest gatehouses in the realm, a 17th century marvel that looks as if it is perpetually basking in the last horizontal rays of a setting sun. Once thought to be the work of Inigo Jones, it is now considered a masterpiece of the Cotswold mason, Timothy Strong of Great Barrington. Stanway House is a Jacobean manor house set in fine gardens surrounded by traditional parkland. It houses a fine display of period furniture. Formerly occupied by the Earl and Countess of Wemyss, several eminent men of letters were guests here - H.G. Wells, Walter de la Mare, G.K. Chesterton, as well as J.M. Barrie, of whom more later. Turn left as you look at the gatehouse, and continue along the road with St Peter's Church on the right. The church was heavily restored in the 19th century but the pulpit is Jacobean.

Opposite the churchyard, where a pair of steps are inserted into its wall, is a series of pretty cottages, washed by a lively stream. Follow the road as it bears right; pass a road and cottages on the left, a tennis court, and, on the right, the magnificent 14th century tithe barn, with its curious eave decoration, like hands poised to throw darts. There is another entrance to Stanway Hall to the right and then, left, a meadow and, beyond it, the cricket pitch and its thatched pavilion resting on staddlestones, a gift from the aforementioned creator of Peter Pan. He was a keen cricketer and on the occasion on his first visit to Stanway he invited the Australians, who were playing at Cheltenham, for a game. Matches at Stanway against visiting elevens became frequent events and within a few years Barrie had left a permanent memorial to the times he enjoyed there with the gift of the pavilion.

On the right, opposite the pavilion, is a stile. Take this and head diagonally left to another stile in a metal fence. After this you will find yourself in tree studded parkland. Bear right towards where two lines of trees have been planted to form an avenue. Between the seventh and eighth tree from the right is a small stake with a yellow arrow on it - head for this. Beyond this stake are two others. Head for these, the land on the right rising gently to a series of hillocks covered in coarse grazing and a few trees, while an old farm building appears to the left. Continue towards a stile which takes you onto the pasture land and then head for another stake in front of you. The view to the left opens up to the dune-like hills. Pass through a metal gate, following the path to the left of a solitary spreading tree. Beyond this the path falls away to hedgerow and a double stile leading to a field of undulating ripples. Once you are in this field, walk across these ripples on a fairly obvious path until you meet another set of stiles, over a stream, which bring you into a gully that rises into a cultivated field. Follow the path on its well-worn right margin. Another stile arrives which takes you into another field of ripples. The roofs of Stanton are clearly visible now - the needle church spire and to its left a red tin barn and to its right a pair of thatched cottages. Head just to the right of the red barn where you will come to a stile set in a metal fence. Cross this and drop onto a paved lane. Turn left and follow this until you reach a road, where you turn right and follow it as it curves left past a singular gibbet-like lantern, ignoring the dead end on the right. This is Stanton, a Cotswold town of eerie perfection.

Pass a couple of thatched cottages on the left and a converted barn with enormous doors to the right. The road bears left but you turn right onto the main street of Stanton, lined with yet more unblemished but ancient Cotswold cottages. Just after the war memorial on the left, a street leads to the Church of St. Michael and All the Angels, which dates back to the 12th century. It boasts a pulpit of unusual antiquity, from about 1375, as well as a Jacobean one, still in use.

Return to the main street and continue towards the tree covered slope before you. Pass the red telephone kiosk on the left, ignore the turning on the right, and head up towards the Mount Inn, which you keep to your left. Behind you is a fine view of the clustered roofs of Stanton.

Beyond the Inn, as the road curves to the left, you will see a path on the far side of the road leading up between hedgerows. Here begins a period of intense ascent. The path brings you to a metal gate which leads onto open, coarse hillside. Immediately you find yourself at the apex of two paths. Take the lesser one on the right. After a short while you will come to another gate. Go through this into a small meadow; bear right past a wooden hut and towards a telegraph pole. Pass through another gate into a field at the far end of which is dense, dark woodland. Once in the field you meet a path. Cross this and head towards a wooden fence where you will find a stile, a wide track and another stile. Cross both stiles, with magnificent views behind, and head down towards the nearest corner of woodland, where you should find a stake pointing the way to a narrow entrance to the wood.

Immediately you enter the wood, turn left and follow a vague path along its left margin. After about fifty yards the path swings right and then left towards a ruined stone barn. Keep the barn to your right whereupon you will meet another path at the base of a steep wooded bank. Turn right, with the length of the barn, rather than its beam, now on your right. Opposite, on your left is a knobbly tree stump. Continue past the barn, with the old stone water trough at the end and ignore the track on the right that leads back into the woods. Take the path before you, which rises a little, and is perfumed by the fragrance of pine trees. This path will soon take you into the woods past a pair of old stone gate posts, one hundred yards after which you will come to a stone wall. Turn left steeply through the remains of a stile, keeping close to the stone wall on the right. After about fifty yards you will come to another track and a metal gate on the right. Go through this and turn directly left, with the stone wall and woodland now to your left, up a scrubby hillside covered with thorn bushes.

The summit offers the best views yet, at your back; but look to your right for a stake and make for it. Turn immediately left at the stake - you will see a farmhouse across the little canyon. Walk towards it by descending to the track, crossing the eye of the loop formed by the track and climbing up the other side to the corner of the fence. Continue forward towards Shenberrow Farm and turn left through a gate onto a track that leads to a row of trees. Just beyond these trees there is a cattle grid on the right and a track that leads back into the farm. Take this. Once you are in the farmyard, heading for an ancient, squeezed timbered farm building, turn left, go through a metal gate, and bear right until the farmhouse appears on the right. Do not follow the blue arrows through the gate ahead of you, but take the track on the left, with the stone wall on the right, and a distant view of Broadway Tower to the left, until you come to a metal gate. Turn right through the gate and then immediately right through a smaller gate. Cross a field diagonally along a clear path to another small gate. Go through this into another field and head for a wooden bridle gate. Once through this, ignore the track on the right into the woods but continue a little to the main track and turn right, heading downhill towards a couple of houses.

Soon, just before the houses, you meet an entrance to the woods on the right. Ignore this but take the next one about twenty yards after and follow the green markers, proceeding across the crossroads you meet after about thirty yards. The path becomes a track and makes a pretty big slash through the woods, plunging ever downwards. After a while you pass a little slip-track on the left, leading to a pump of some kind. Ignore this and at the complicated junction soon after carry straight on, ignoring all turnings to left and right. Immediately after that the path forks - the path on the right leads to a farm, whilst the left fork, which you want, takes you past a cool green glade of slender trees.

Soon the track veers left but you should take the narrow path that leads off it to the right. This is narrow and may be muddy, although this can be avoided with care. Eventually you will fetch up at the main road, the B4077. Turn right and, keeping to the path, walk along the road for about a quarter of a mile, past some cottages and a fine telephone box until you see a path sign on the right. You enter a sort of orchard. Head to the right of a stone wall, with a stream on the left, and pass through a kissing gate, delightfully decorated with the carved head of a swan. On your left is a lodge, on the right is Stanway House. Continue to the road past a fir with seats around its base and turn right until you see the Gatehouse.

The STANWAY/STANTON Walk

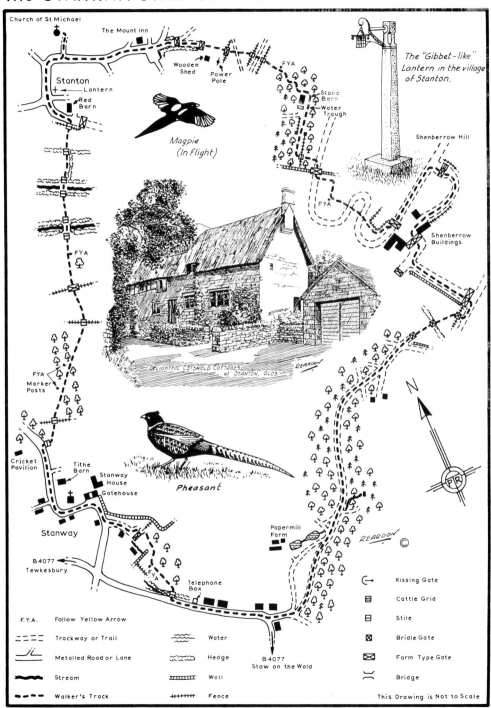

Church of St Michael

The Mount Inn

Wooden Shed

Power Pole

Stanton

Lantern

Red Barn

FYA

Stone Barn

Water Trough

The "Gibbet-like" Lantern in the village of Stanton.

Shenberrow Hill

Shenberrow Buildings

Magpie (In Flight)

FYA

FYA Marker Posts

DELIGHTFUL COTSWOLD COTTAGES at STANTON, GLOS

REARDON

Cricket Pavilion

Tithe Barn

Stanway House

Gatehouse

Stanway

Pheasant

N

B 4077 Tewkesbury

Papermill Farm

REARDON ©

FYA

Telephone Box

B 4077 Stow on the Wold

	Kissing Gate
	Cattle Grid
	Stile
	Bridle Gate
	Farm Type Gate
	Bridge

F.Y.A.   Follow Yellow Arrow

– – – –   Trackway or Trail   ～～～ Water

‿‿   Metalled Road or Lane   ⌇⌇⌇⌇ Hedge

▬▬   Stream   ▨▨▨▨ Wall

▬ ▬ ▬   Walker's Track   +++++ Fence

This Drawing is Not to Scale

35

9. Daneway

Distance: 5 miles
Time: 2½/2¾ hours of uninterrupted walking
Map: SO 80/90 (Stroud area) in the OS Pathfinder series
Starting Point: Grid reference 939034
Terrain: Mostly track and field with a little road walking. One or two places are likely to be very muddy but on the whole the going is firm and although there are a couple of steep ascents they are mercifully brief.
Refreshments: Daneway Inn.

THIS walk starts close to the Daneway Inn, just outside the village of Sapperton, on the fringes of the Golden Valley. The area is noted for the Old Thames and Severn Canal, the banks of which form part of this walk. The countryside of the area is a mix of the wild and the ordered, a series of steep and tangled little valleys, a contrast to the generally open areas of the Cotswolds.

Parking is not too easy here unless you plan to patronise the Daneway Inn, which has a spacious car park. The Inn, and the few other dwellings here, are wedged into one of the plunging little valleys characteristic of this part of the Cotswolds. The Inn stands on the corner of the road not far from the end of the old canal tunnel and in fact was built for the refreshment of the 'leggers' who propelled the barges through the two miles of tunnel by lying on their backs and heaving on the ceiling with their feet. However, the walk takes you away from the canal for the time being - follow the road around the Inn in the direction of Miserden and Edgeworth. The road ascends a little here, bears to the left slightly and after about two hundred yards comes to Daneway House on the right. On the left here is the beginning of a signposted footpath. Go over the stile and follow the path as it curves to the left until, after about fifty yards, you will meet a sort of clearing and a choice of gates. Ignore the one on the left and take instead the one to the right that brings you to a path that leads to the crest of the hill. As you puff up the hill towards a line of trees take time to look at the scenes around you - Daneway House becomes more clearly visible behind and the eccentric topography of the area, with its sharp declivities and miniature canyons, more obvious. The village of Sapperton, where poet John Masefield resided during the Second World War, will become visible behind you.

At the top you will find yourself on a wide, flat swathe of land, the beginning of a plateau. Directly ahead of you, about fifty yards away, you will see a gate set into a stone wall. Pass through this onto the edge of a stony field and an utter change in the landscape, from windswept scruffiness to the uncluttered order of cultivated land. There is a hedge on the left, filled with bobbing and chirruping birds. Walk forward keeping to the left hand margin of the field, for some considerable time, with the grey roof of a farm building gradually rising out of the horizon to the right, as the land gently undulates, until the field spreads out to the left. Continue to follow the hedge as it describes a semi-circle and continue forward.

The hedge comes to an end and views open up to the left, with a slender church spire in the distance. The end of the field is marked by the appearance of Tunley Cottage. Go through the gate and pass to the right of the cottage with its stained glass, and drop down into the lane. Turn left and follow the road for about forty yards until it falls away to the left while a track leading to Tunley House runs off to the right, (but straight ahead of you as you approach it). Keep to the track, as it curves slightly to the right. Cottages appear to the right. Ignore the gate you will pass on the right and a lane that passes between two large Cedar trees. Head instead for Tunley House ahead of you and enter the farmyard, passing a solitary stone arch with wooden door on the left. Immediately you are in the yard, bear right, following a stone wall and passing an old farm building with attractive arched windows.

Go through the gap between this building and another to the left and follow the stony path that descends left through the trees. Continue down until you meet a stream and beyond it, a gate to the right. Do not cross the stream or the gate but turn left up through the trees for about twenty yards so that you are once again level with the farm yard.

THE CHURCH OF ST KENELM, IN A TRULY COTSWOLD SETTING IN THE VILLAGE of SAPPERTON, GLOS.

37

Once you are level with the cottage, bear right at a coppiced tree with several fingers pointing up to the sky. Then head downwards and slightly to the left, with a bank falling away to the right. The path takes you through a gap in the wooden fence and then down fairly steeply through the trees curling left until you emerge onto a green, ribbed field, with Tunley House Farm now above and behind you. The right of way on the OS map rather oddly heads across the field to the road and then turns back upon itself but, more simply, once you are in the field turn right and follow the wood on the right, still below Tunley House Farm, until you see the levelled remains of a stone wall in front of you. There are but few landmarks here - you will have to feel your way slightly here but cross the wall remains and turn immediately left, with woodland above you to the right. Continue walking until you come to a stream which you may cross with the help of some handily laid planks.

Head straight on, a wooden fence appearing to the left, until you see a bridle gate leading into evenly planted woodland. Enter the wood and follow the path on the right margin until you come to a narrow bridge with handrails, followed by a simple plank bridge. Cross both and turn immediately right. Keep to the path as it follows the stream and then begins to climb up away from it. Eventually you will meet another path coming in from the left but keep straight on, passing a bridle gate and cottage on the left, and follow the path as it descends to meet the stream once again. At a corner you will come to another path. Turn left fairly steeply up into the woods, ignoring the stone bridge on the right. The path levels out and you will soon come to a stile, which you cross, at a point where you will see two houses to the right. The path ascends slightly again and joins another path - keep going forward, passing close to one of the houses seen earlier, and cross a stile. Again, continue forward, the track now a road passing between the cottages of Waterlane with their pretty, well tended gardens.

When you reach the main road, cross straight over, following the sign to Oakridge Lynch. After about one hundred yards turn left along the bridlepath, poorly signposted, towards Far Oakridge.

Here the countryside is more open and flat again. After about one hundred and fifty yards you pass a farm on the left, after which the track narrows and later descends to a bottom, rises up as suddenly and then passes a stile on the left, which you ignore. Instead continue forward, passing an old farm building on the right, until you come to a main road. Cross over and follow the narrow lane for Iles Green, the views to the left opening up towards Sapperton. The road curves left around the very attractive Iles House of 1614 with its terraced gardens and mysterious topiary, and soon comes to a Y junction. Take the right arm, marked as a No Through Road and as unsuitable for motors.

The road becomes a gully between two hedges clipped with brutal efficiency, with a hillside of tangled trees ahead of you. The road continues to taper until by Trillis Cottage it declines to a steep and stony track. It takes you around a corner to reveal two small man-made lakes. Then, by now a path, it descends around the water and into woodland. Ignore the path on your left, on the other side of the lakes. Very soon a red brick bridge will appear in front of you over what remains of the the old Thames and Severn Canal which was in use between 1789 and 1911. Cross the bridge and turn immediately left, following the right bank of the canal, with the River Frome to the right. Follow the path and a series of locks until, after about a quarter of a mile a narrow bridge takes you to the other bank. Bear right and continue until you meet a cluster of houses and emerge on to the road opposite the Daneway Inn for a well deserved drink.

The DANEWAY Walk

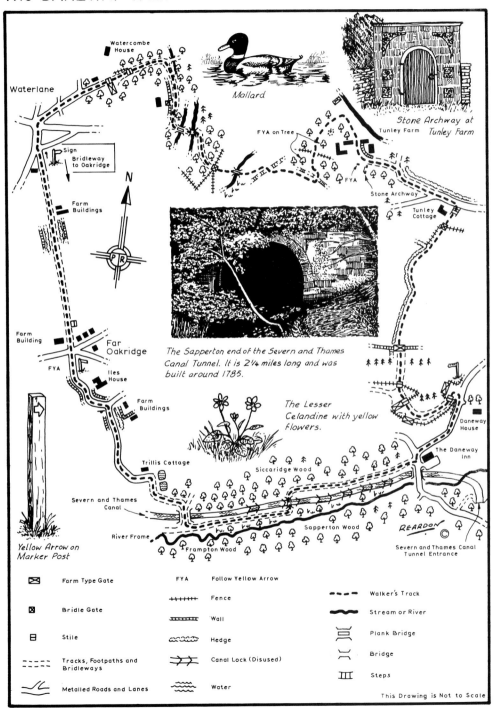

Watercombe House

Mallard

Stone Archway at Tunley Farm

Tunley Farm

Waterlane

FYA on Tree

Sign Bridleway to Oakridge

FYA

Stone Archway

N

Farm Buildings

Tunley Cottage

The Sapperton end of the Severn and Thames Canal Tunnel. It is 2¼ miles long and was built around 1785.

Farm Building

Far Oakridge

FYA

Iles House

Farm Buildings

The Lesser Celandine with yellow flowers.

Daneway House

The Daneway Inn

Trillis Cottage

Siccaridge Wood

Severn and Thames Canal

Sapperton Wood

REARDON ©

River Frome

Frampton Wood

Severn and Thames Canal Tunnel Entrance

Yellow Arrow on Marker Post

⊠ Farm Type Gate	FYA	Follow Yellow Arrow	▪▪▪▪ Walker's Track
⊡ Bridle Gate	+++++	Fence	～～ Stream or River
🞒 Stile	▭▭▭	Wall	Plank Bridge
---- Tracks, Footpaths and Bridleways	⌒⌒⌒⌒	Hedge	Bridge
⌇⌇ Metalled Roads and Lanes	⇉⇉	Canal Lock (Disused)	Ⅲ Steps
	～～～	Water	This Drawing is Not to Scale

10. Coln St Aldwyn/Bibury

Distance: 5.5 miles
Time: 2.5 hours of uninterrupted walking
Map: OS Pathfinder SP 00/10 (Cirencester)
Starting point: grid reference 147051. Near the New Inn in Coln St Aldwyn.
Terrain: Meadow and field, farm track and riverside paths for the most part. The walk is almost wholly even, with two or three sharp, but very short, ascents or descents.
Refreshments: Excellent food at the New Inn in Coln St Aldwyn, the Catherine Wheel in Bibury and at the Bibury tea shop.

THIS walk is fractionally longer than usual but the good news is that it is essentially on the flat. Furthermore it takes you to one of the Gloucestershire villages that is a byword for Cotswold beauty: Bibury, much visited by car but less so, perhaps, by foot. Since you are sure to want to linger in Bibury you must allow more time than is allotted above, which is for the walk itself.

Before commencing the walk you may wish to visit the church on the other side of the village. With a history of 700 years, the church, curiously dedicated to the Decollation of St. John, is notable for its pretty location, surrounded as it is by charming cottages bedecked in flowers and rows of ancient gravestones. The tower has some interesting gargoyles on the outside and although the interior is plain, there are some attractive windows at the east end dedicated to the Keble family of great repute.

Turn left out of the New Inn and walk along the road towards the River Coln. The road soon curves to the right and crosses the river for the first time, passing the nineteenth century mill on the right and offering a glimpse of a decorative wooden bridge on the left, among the trees. The road straightens and makes its way between meadows, with the river away to the left and the church tower peeping over the trees to the right, towards a pair of cottages standing guard over another bridge. Cross this little bump of a bridge and turn off the road, right, to pass through the grounds of the smaller cottage which will now be on your left.

Go through the gate ahead of you to find yourself in a meadow with the river running off to your right. There are two signposts here - one points in the direction of the river whilst the other, marked bridle path, is the one you require. This points roughly ahead and left, towards some isolated trees, among them a startling copper beech.

Keep to the right of these trees, the path rising very slightly towards woodland on your left. Pretty soon you arrive at a stone wall on the margin of the wood where you turn right and pass through a gate into another meadow. Ignore the gate into the woods on the left, the site of a disused quarry. Strike out ahead of you towards a farm building you see in the far distance, beyond several fields. There is a sharp drop below you on the right and trees beyond.

Eventually you will reach another gate which will bring you onto the edge of a field. If the corn is still standing, the path will nonetheless be an obvious furrow straight ahead of you. Wade through this golden sea towards the barn. As you approach the edge of this field a large house will appear to your right and the path may veer slightly to the right towards the entrance to the next field ahead of you. Here again the path is straight before you. Aim to the right of the barn and to the left of a cottage opposite it. At the other end of the field is a gate. Go through this onto a track which you cross and continue straight ahead with the cottage to your right, heading for a gate in front of you and slightly to the left.

Go through the gate into another field and head across it diagonally to the left, keeping to the right of the spreading oak tree, towards a house set into the corner of the field, the trees to the right of it looking like a belch of green smoke. Some twenty five yards before this house there is a gate in the hedge on the left. Go through this spring loaded gate onto a lane and turn right.

Pass the house on your right, which has a coat of arms on its front, and then another, ignoring the lane running between them. Continue along the lane until you quickly come to a green sign indicating a footpath on the right. Take this stony track, flanked by young planted trees on the left, with blackberry bushes between them, and acres of cereal on the right. The track dips down and passes through a gate in a stone wall into a coarse meadow, with woodland ahead of you. Very soon after entering the field you will be crossing the all but invisible route of the old Roman road, Akeman Street, which once linked Cirencester with Bicester. Within one hundred yards of entering the field there is vague evidence of the imprint of a track running athwart you.

The track takes you down between two shoulders of a hill towards a gate after which the track, hemmed in by bushes, rises again. Ignore the field on the left, keeping on the track next to the stone wall on the right. As you proceed the track becomes the edge of the field and behind you the long limbs of the firs in the woodland become visible.

The track continues clearly across cultivated land. Soon a barn will appear to your right and soon after a track leading up to it, which you ignore. Continue to the end of the field and pass through a gateway with tall, bushy hedge on your left and views of the countryside far ahead. Soon the roofs of Bibury will appear to your right and then the field ends and you pass through another gateway. At the end of this field there is a crossroads with, perhaps affixed to the gatepost on the left a small sign giving directions. You want to turn right here, between the margins of two fields and head for Bibury and the houses you will have noted earlier. You pass through another gateway to another field, more of Bibury appearing both ahead of you and below you to the left. Then you will arrive at a wooden gate and several choices of route - keep straight ahead and pass through a metal gate onto a track. This will take you down between some attractive cottages to your left and right - the first on the right was restored in 1971, the second has a set of stone steps leading to a blank wall. You will quickly arrive at a narrow lane with severe yellow lines at the kerb. Continue forward across the little green and bear right, steeply downwards.

You will emerge alongside Arlington Row on your right, one of the most famous collection of cottages in the country. Low, with quaint gables, these are a delightful example of 17th century wool weavers' cottages. Opposite them to your left is the wetland of Rack Isle, so called because wool was formerly hung up to dry here. Bibury has been mentioned by distinguished men of letters. Alexander Pope wrote to

Swift in 1726, "I shall never more think of...the woods of Ciceter or the pleasing prospect of Byberry, but your Idea must be join'd with 'em". The diarist John Byng, 5th Viscount Torrington wrote of a stay there in 1794 "After breakfast and two fine basins of snail tea which always is of sovereign use to my lungs, we walked down the village, by the side of a pastoral trout stream full of fish, (for this place is a famous spot for fly-fishing...). We procured the key of the church (a key the size of Dover Castle) and admired it as lightstone, and well-glazed." By continuing to the road and turning right you may visit the church with its Anglo-Saxon remains; or turn left for the Swan Hotel and the Arlington Mill Museum and Trout Farm. For those, however, who wish to continue the walk, turn right immediately after the cottages, over a stone slab stile, cross a sort of courtyard and bear right behind the cottages and up a set of wide steps to the edge of a wood. At the top you are presented with a cool, clear path straight ahead of you through the woods which will lead you to another slab stile and leave you in a field.

Ahead of you is a wooden building. Aim just to the left of this, the cricket pavilion, and the wooden fence that surrounds the pitch, and then bear to the right, heading for the top right hand corner of the field, where there is a stile at the edge of the woods. This leads onto a path which skirts the woods and descends to the left. Soon you reach a stile. Go over this and into a field from which you then cross onto a wide track, with a meadow and woodland, skirted by the Coln, in front of you, and a grand house to the left. Turn right here and, ignoring any track that may invite you towards the river, head up the slope until you come to a junction where you turn left. Keep walking until a point where the track sweeps up to the right - ignore this and walk straight ahead, with the woods on your left, onto another track. As the path descends slightly, pass through a wooden gate into a field. Keep to the left hand margin, pass through another gate, and then another, after which there is a sharp drop to a stone slab stile. Cross this into a meadow and bear slightly left around the base of a wooded hillock which will bring you to a gate and the river. You are now on a grassy track, with woodland to your right. Pass through another gate, by which time you are very close to the limpid River Coln. The river, overlooked by fields on the far bank, meanders off again as you continue forward in a field with a steepish slope on the right. As the river comes and goes fishermen stand patiently, looking hopefully into the water; waterfowl, from swan to moorhen, sidle among the rushes.

After about a quarter of a mile pass through a gate and continue forwards. Fairly soon you will come to a point where a possible track may seduce you across a field to the right towards woodland. Ignore this but pass into a small neighbouring field and then bear right, leaving the river behind, along a fairly obvious path in such a way that you will find yourself on the left edge of the wood. Soon a house will appear above you some distance in front.

The path then bears right into the woods. Follow it for a short while until you re-emerge through a gate into a meadow where the path is fairly obvious in front of you and the river on your left. Shortly a familiar cottage will appear on your left - pass through the gate onto the road, turn left and return to where you started.

The COLN St ALDWYN – BIBURY Walk

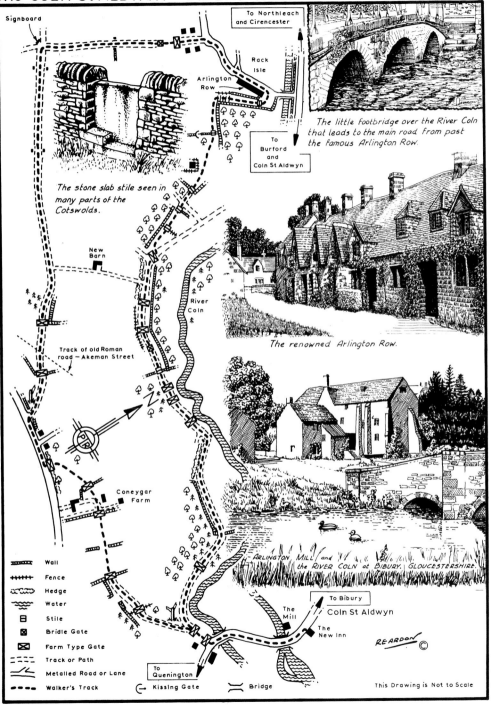

Signboard

To Northleach
and Cirencester

Rack Isle

Arlington Row

To Burford and Coln St Aldwyn

The little footbridge over the River Coln
that leads to the main road from past
the famous Arlington Row.

The stone slab stile seen in
many parts of the
Cotswolds.

New Barn

River Coln

Track of old Roman
road – Akeman Street

The renowned Arlington Row.

Coneygar Farm

ARLINGTON MILL and
the RIVER COLN at BIBURY, GLOUCESTERSHIRE.

The Mill

To Bibury

Coln St Aldwyn

The New Inn

REARDON ©

To Quenington

⚏⚏⚏	Wall
┼┼┼┼	Fence
⌒⌒⌒	Hedge
〜〜〜	Water
⊟	Stile
⊠	Bridle Gate
⊠	Farm Type Gate
- - -	Track or Path
—✦—	Metalled Road or Lane
• • •	Walker's Track
⟲	Kissing Gate
⟆	Bridge

This Drawing is Not to Scale

INDEX